W9-BFN-951

THE BOYS' BOOK OF SPYCRAFT

HOW TO BE THE BEST SECRET AGENT EVER

Written by Martin Oliver
Illustrated by Simon Ecob

With thanks to Sally Pilkington and Anton Dalby

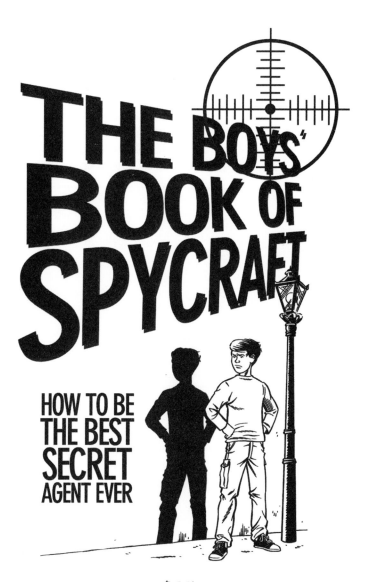

THE BOYS' BOOK OF BOOK OF SPYCRAFT

HOW TO BE THE BEST SECRET AGENT EVER

PSS!
PRICE STERN SLOAN
An Imprint of Penguin Group (USA) Inc.

DISCLAIMER

The publisher disclaims, as far as is legally permissible, all liability
for accidents, injuries, or loss that may occur as a result of the
information or instructions given in this book. Use common sense
at all times—always wear appropriate safety gear, be very careful
with scissors, and be considerate of other people.

PRICE STERN SLOAN
Published by the Penguin Group
Penguin Group (USA) Inc., 375 Hudson Street, New York, New York 10014, USA
Penguin Group (Canada), 90 Eglinton Avenue East, Suite 700,
Toronto, Ontario M4P 2Y3, Canada
(a division of Pearson Penguin Canada Inc.)
Penguin Books Ltd., 80 Strand, London WC2R 0RL, England
Penguin Group Ireland, 25 St. Stephen's Green, Dublin 2, Ireland
(a division of Penguin Books Ltd.)
Penguin Group (Australia), 250 Camberwell Road, Camberwell, Victoria 3124, Australia
(a division of Pearson Australia Group Pty. Ltd.)
Penguin Books India Pvt. Ltd., 11 Community Center,
Panchsheel Park, New Delhi—110 017, India
Penguin Group (NZ), 67 Apollo Drive, Rosedale, Auckland 0632, New Zealand
(a division of Pearson New Zealand Ltd.)
Penguin Books (South Africa) (Pty.) Ltd., 24 Sturdee Avenue,
Rosebank, Johannesburg 2196, South Africa

Penguin Books Ltd., Registered Offices: 80 Strand, London WC2R 0RL, England

The scanning, uploading, and distribution of this book via the Internet or via any other means without the
permission of the publisher is illegal and punishable by law. Please purchase only authorized electronic
editions and do not participate in or encourage electronic piracy of copyrighted materials. Your support of
the author's rights is appreciated.

Copyright © 2009 Buster Books. First published in Great Britain by Buster Books, an imprint of Michael
O'Mara Books Limited. First published in the United States in 2011 by Price Stern Sloan, a division of
Penguin Young Readers Group, 345 Hudson Street, New York, New York 10014. *PSS!* is a registered
trademark of Penguin Group (USA) Inc. Printed in the U.S.A.

ISBN 978-0-8431-9846-1   10 9 8 7 6 5 4 3 2 1

CONTENTS

SAFE SPYING

The hints and tips in this book are intended for practice purposes only. A good spy should always keep his wits about him, so keep in mind that some ideas in this book are intended purely to help you *imagine* what it might be like to join James Bond on a top secret mission. **Under no circumstances should you ever attempt any exercise that would put you or anyone else in any danger in real life.**

We urge you, at all times, to make yourself aware of, and obey, all laws, regulations, and local by-laws, and respect all rights, including the rights of property owners. Always respect other people's privacy and remember to ask responsible adults for assistance and take their advice whenever necessary.

Above all, remember to use common sense and to take all necessary safety precautions when preparing to attempt any project, particularly when using heat or sharp objects. That said, it is fun to learn new skills that may one day prove useful, so get ready to enter the secret world of spycraft!

HOW TO SET UP A SPY RING

Although some spies prefer to work alone, it's a lot more fun to build your headquarters, plan operations, and trade messages with a group of friends. What you need to do is set up your own "spy ring." A spy ring is an undercover organization run by a "spy master" along with several "field agents" and a "go-between." Keep reading to learn more about these roles and how to recruit friends into your organization.

Spy Master: The person who sets up a spy ring is called the spy master. This is the most important role in a spy ring—this is a job for you! The spy master is the person who chooses missions, decides on strategy, and directs operations. A spy master's identity must be kept secret at all times.

Field Agents: Next there are field agents—spies who are in the "field" carrying out missions. A field agent does the exciting and difficult jobs, such as staking out suspects, passing along information, and mounting surveillance operations.

Go-Between: The final person in a spy ring is the go-between, who passes communications between the spy master and the field agents. The go-between is a level above a field agent because he must be capable of acting as an active spy as well as being an excellent communicator.

STEP ONE

Your first step as spy master is to choose a suitable go-between. Pick someone you trust, but try not to be too obvious by picking your best friend—that could easily blow your cover.

Approach your potential go-between and discuss the idea of a spy ring with him. Don't identify yourself as the spy master. Just casually mention that you've heard that someone is setting up a secret club that sounds like it might be fun. Gauge your friend's reaction—if he seems interested, describe the role of the go-between. Why not say that you'd love to be chosen for that role? This helps to cover your identity as spy master or as someone already involved in the ring at all.

STEP TWO

If your friend says that he would like the job of go-between, wait a few days, then tell him you have been told to give him the task of recruiting up to four field agents. You could even allow yourself to be recruited, so that you have the fun of being a field agent while also protecting your real identity as the spy master.

THE RULES

Now it's time to learn some spy ring rules:

• Keep the number of members in your spy ring to between four and six. If too many people are involved you increase the risk of discovery.

• Any communication between the members of the ring should be in code (you will find a variety of suitable codes in this book).

• Make sure that during a mission all your agents are not working together at any one time. If you are discovered together, your spy ring can be blown wide open. Operate in twos and threes.

• Ideally, as spy master, you should be the only one to know the identities of all the members of the ring and their roles. This way, if an agent is discovered and interrogated, he will not put your entire operation in jeopardy by naming other operatives. However, this won't be much fun for your friends and will make meetings very hard, so you may have to break this rule!

HOW TO SET UP
YOUR HEADQUARTERS

You've probably noticed that in spy films and books the characters are often multimillionaires, with a secret cave or hideaway as their headquarters. If you don't have the funds for an underground cave complex, don't worry! With a little careful planning, you can create a highly effective base for the espionage activities you'll soon be masterminding.

AWAY FROM PRYING EYES

A spy's headquarters should always be top secret. If you have a backyard you could build a camouflaged den (see pages

29–30). However, your bedroom, set up correctly, will make an excellent headquarters.

Here are the important elements to include when setting up the perfect spy HQ in your bedroom:

• Your HQ should have a floor area large enough to lie down on. This will be useful for practicing sit-ups and push-ups to improve your basic fitness—essential for the best spies—before you attempt an obstacle course (see pages 40–42).

• Your HQ must include a desk at which to plan missions. A desk offers plenty of hiding places for secret documents, as well as providing ample room to create anti-snooping devices and space for mastering code-breaking techniques (see pages 120–121).

Spy Tip: Make sure you are seen sitting at your desk doing homework regularly, so no one questions what you are doing when you are sitting at it.

• A mirror is a vital piece of equipment for many reasons. You will be able to use it when creating a disguise and to check your appearance before leaving HQ. It will also provide defense against surprise visits (see page 14). The best kind of mirror to get is one on a stand so you can adjust it depending on whether you are using it to put on disguises or to keep an eye on the door to your HQ.

• Hang a framed picture on the wall—a photograph of you looking your best is always nice. On the front is an innocent-looking you—on the reverse, attach a clear plastic document folder into which you can slip the outline of your latest mission or coded messages that need to be broken. Simply flip the picture over according to who is in HQ at the time.

• Buy a map of your local area. This is invaluable for plotting the route of your missions. If your bedroom window has a roller blind, pull it down and secure the map to the front of it—just pull the cord to make it disappear in a flash. Alternatively, stick your map to a sheet of cardboard that can be slipped under your bed when not in use.

OTHER ESSENTIAL ITEMS

a flashlight • a small notebook
• some pens and pencils
• pieces of paper and cardstock
• paintbrushes • sticky tack • adhesive tape
• chalk • scissors • small mirrors
• talcum powder
• junk, such as tin cans, toilet paper rolls,
juice cartons, rope
• unusual clothing for disguises
(a collection of coats, hats, scarves)
• dark sunglasses

USEFUL, BUT NONESSENTIAL ITEMS

a computer
• a camera phone
• face paints
• a tarp or bedsheet
• a pair of binoculars

HOW TO SET UP AN ADVANCE WARNING SYSTEM

As a spy, security is one of your top priorities. To keep your secrets safe, it's vital to stay on the lookout for "unfriendlies" (siblings, parents, and rival agents). A few seconds' warning may be all you have to ensure you aren't taken by surprise. Use any of these simple precautions to protect your HQ:

- Balance an empty tin can on the doorknob inside the room. Anyone trying to open the door will dislodge the can, warning you of a potential intruder and giving you time to conceal secret files.

- Angle a mirror so that you always have a view of the door to your room. This way no one can sneak up on you.

- Keep your HQ dimly lit and the light in the hallway outside your room on. This will help you to keep an eye out for shadows under the door, created by anyone standing behind it listening.

HOW TO SET UP A BALANCE ALARM

A balance alarm will guarantee that any snoops are uncovered.

You will need:

3 toilet paper rolls • 3 different colored pens or pencils

1. Number the toilet paper rolls, 1 through 3, so you can identify them.

2. Stand the rolls just behind the door to HQ as you leave.

3. Balance a pen or pencil on top of each roll. Note which color pen is on which of the numbered toilet paper rolls and the order of the numbers from left to right.

4. When you return to base, you will be able to tell if anyone has been inside, knocked over the balance alarm, and tried to cover their tracks. It's very unlikely that the toilet paper rolls will be in the correct order right to left, with the correct pen or pencil on top.

Spy Tip: Vary the combinations each time you use this alarm.

15

HOW TO POINT THE FINGER AT AN INTRUDER

The most dangerous time for your HQ is when you are away from it. If you think someone may try to infiltrate HQ, use these measures:

• Pull a hair from your head and drench it in spit. As you leave your HQ, close the door behind you and stick the damp hair across the space between the door and the doorframe. If anyone goes in while you are out, the hair will fall and you'll know you've had a "visitor."

• If you have a camera phone, take a photo of your HQ each time you leave. When you get back, compare the picture with the scene in front of you. Try to spot differences that indicate someone has been rifling through your stuff.

• Maintain top-level security by keeping spy files in alphabetical order—except for one. A rival rooting through will probably put them all back in perfect alphabetical order—a major snoop alert.

If you think your HQ has been penetrated, here's a great way to track down the culprit:

1. Sprinkle talcum powder in the doorway to your HQ—a fine layer on the carpet or floor that an intruder won't notice.

2. When you return, check the floor for footprints. If anyone has trespassed, they will have left tracks in the powder. Check the shoes in the closets of everyone in your household for talcum powder on the soles. You will soon have the culprit!

POINTING THE FINGER

Whenever you touch an object with your bare hands, tiny amounts of sweat and oil from your skin are left behind as fingerprints. These are identical copies of the ridged patterns on your fingertips. No two people have the same fingerprints, which means you can compile a record of the prints left after any break-ins and hopefully use them to find out exactly who has entered your spy HQ.

The key to lifting a copy of a fingerprint from a surface is to use a fine powder that will stick to the greasy residue left behind. This will enable you to take a "print." Here's how to become an expert print analyst.

You will need:

a paintbrush • adhesive tape
• a pencil • a pencil sharpener • a nail file
• a sheet of white paper

1. Make your own fingerprint dust with a pencil and nail file by sharpening the pencil then rubbing away at the graphite point with the file. This gives you a dark-colored powder, or graphite dust, which will show up against the white paper.

2. Sprinkle the graphite dust lightly over the suspect's fingerprint.

3. Gently use your brush to spread out the graphite dust until you see the fingerprint becoming visible. If you can't see any prints, use the dust to explore different areas of your HQ to find some. It might take a little while, but don't give up. Think about where the intruder may have put his or her hands—places like  the doorknob or a drawer handle. This process is known as "dusting for prints."

4. Once you've found a fingerprint, you need to capture, catalog, and identify it. To do this, place a piece of tape, sticky-side down, over the print. Make sure that the tape is large enough to cover the whole print. Press firmly on the tape over the print, then carefully peel it off again. You should be able to see the print clearly on the tape.

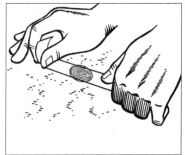

5. Stick the tape containing the print onto a sheet of white paper and label it with details of where and when it was found.

6. Identify the owner of the print (and of the intruder) by checking it against the prints of your friends and members of your family. Get them to press each of their fingertips onto a clean, shiny surface and take their prints using the method just described.

Why not plan ahead and create a book of the prints of people who are often in your bedroom? In an emergency, you can compare a suspect's print against the prints in your book to make a positive match more quickly.

Spy Tip: If you're going to use this method, it's a good idea to clean the surface of your desk and the fronts of your drawers with a damp cloth before leaving your HQ. This cleans the scene and ensures your fingerprints or older prints do not confuse the situation.

HOW TO HAVE THE BEST SECRET HIDING PLACES

Ideally, you would be able to flip a switch and make the walls of your HQ rotate so that all of your secret spy equipment instantly disappeared from sight. Unfortunately, this doesn't tend to happen in the real world.

You'll need to find the perfect hiding places for your codebooks, spy lists, and reports to keep them safe from prying eyes, double agents, or, worst of all, your mom!

IN PLAIN SIGHT

If you ever have to hide a file quickly, it is essential to already have a good hiding place in mind. The messier your HQ is, the easier it will be to hide things "in plain sight." This means that a file can be right under a snooper's nose without them noticing it.

However, if your parents have a clean-room rule, here are some alternative suggestions for slipping things out of sight in a split second:

- Slide secret papers underneath a rug, between books on your bookshelves, or under your mattress. Tape a clear plastic folder (the kind people put sheets of paper in to keep them safe) to the underside of a drawer. You can easily slip papers in and out of these places.

- When you're working on an important, secret e-mail or text document, open a second, innocent-looking "decoy" window on your computer's desktop. Make sure the decoy window is large enough to conceal the whole desktop. If you're interrupted, "hot-switch" to your decoy window by using "alt" + "tab" for a PC ("⌘" + "tab" if you are using a Macintosh computer).

• Fold your papers up small enough to fit inside a stinky sneaker, put them inside, and cover with a smelly sock to repel snoopers.

• Tape any sensitive material to the back of a framed picture—only the most professional enemy agent will think to look there.

These ideas are great for short-term solutions, but all good spies play the "long game," which means preparing in advance to create a secure and permanent hiding place. It takes a bit more effort, but it will pay off in the end—there are great long-term solutions throughout this book.

HOW TO SPOT A GOOD SPY

The most successful espionage agents are so good at what they do that it's virtually impossible to tell that they are spies at all. Whether you're an agent working alone or looking for new recruits, you need to know the qualities that make some people better at spycraft than others.

Use the following questions to check your own potential spy skills or to distinguish high-quality individuals from the crowd.

CAN YOUR SUBJECT KEEP A SECRET?

If you suspect your "subject" (the person you are considering recruiting) is a bit of a blabbermouth, ask a fellow agent to test the subject with fake information. The agent should tell him a "secret" such as:

"My brother has an extra toe," or "Michael has green pee."

If, next time you see him, your subject can't resist telling you what he's heard, you'll know he finds it hard to keep quiet and may not be the best person to join your operation.

IS YOUR SUBJECT OBSERVANT?

All good spies have to keep their eyes and ears open at all times. You never know when you might come across an important piece of information or take a suspect by surprise. Even the smallest detail can turn out to be the key to successfully completing a mission. Test your subject's observational skills with the memory tests on pages 31–32. Anyone who doesn't pass the tests shouldn't make the cut.

IS YOUR SUBJECT FIT AND ACTIVE?

Superspies are certainly no couch potatoes. They need to be fit, active, and ready for anything in case they are sent on dangerous missions.

It is important to know whether your subjects can keep up.

- Can they swim?
- Can they ride a bike or skateboard?
- Can they tie knots?
- Can they ski?

The more skills a recruit can master, the better.

If subjects don't score very highly in this area, suggest that they take up a sport, such as swimming or running, to build up their strength and stamina. Any race against time will be tough for an out-of-shape agent.

IS YOUR SUBJECT ABLE TO IMPROVISE?

One of the most exciting things about being a spy is the unpredictable nature of your life. You never know what might happen and where you might end up. This means that the ability to improvise (this means to think quickly and work with whatever is around you at the time) is vital. See how your recruits deal with the unexpected by giving them the action challenge on pages 60–62.

IS YOUR SUBJECT INCONSPICUOUS?

A great spy can easily blend into the background, but this will never happen if your potential recruit has bright pink hair, a ring through his nose, or a tattoo on his forehead.

A good disguise can work wonders, but if a recruit has highly distinguishing features, it will be much trickier to make him look inconspicuous. Average-looking people often make better spies as they find it easier to go "incognito." Natural show-offs draw attention to themselves—they may stand out too much and be unsuited to serious spying.

Make an assessment sheet for your dossier and grade potential recruits out of ten in each of the categories listed below.

SKILLS ASSESSMENT SHEET

Use the points below to figure out how well-suited your recruit is in becoming a trainee spy. Grade recruits out of ten for each skill—a score of 30 or above means that they could make a useful addition to your spy ring.

1. The ability to keep things to himself.

2. Good attention to detail.

3. Keeps in good physical and mental shape.

4. The ability to blend in with the crowd.

5. The ability to think on his feet and deal with the unexpected.

HOW TO CREATE THE PERFECT COVER STORY

If people begin to get suspicious about all the activity in your spy HQ or see you rummaging around in the bushes at your local park and wonder why, you'll need to create a cover story to explain your strange behavior. The right story will stop people from worrying what you're up to and provide a reasonable excuse for what you are doing at the same time.

Here are some suggestions:

• Claim that you've formed a wildlife club. There's nothing you enjoy more than studying animal antics in the local park! This way you can carry out "dead-letter drops" (see pages 46–48) again and again without drawing suspicion.

• Announce that you and your friends have started a book group—this gives everyone in your spy ring a great reason for being in spy HQ all the time. Just remind everyone to bring matching books on each visit!

• Tell people that you and your friends are helping one another study. Make sure that agents bring real homework when they visit your house to prove this.

CODE NAME COVER-UP

Give each agent a code name that is linked to your cover story to add credibility. For example, if you tell everyone that you are in a wildlife club, each agent's code name could be a particular animal or bird, such as: "Hawk," "Fox," or "Snake."

If your cover story is a book group, why not give each agent the name of a favorite writer? Your code names could include: "Pullman," "Rowling," and "Dahl."

Or, if you decided to tell people that your spy ring is a study group, each agent's code name could refer to their "best subject," such as math ("Number-cruncher"), science ("Physics-whiz"), or English ("Word-wizard").

DRESS UP!

If you are caught on a mission in full disguise by a close friend or member of your family who recognizes you, it is essential to always carry a fake invite to a costume party. All you need to do is pull out the invite and announce you are on the way to the party to explain your strange appearance.

HOW TO CREATE A QUICK DISGUISE

Even as a trainee spy, you should already be thinking about how to think and behave as a spy—starting with your outfits. Your spy kit should contain at least one item that can be used if you realize you are being tailed at any point on a mission. It should be something that will instantly change your appearance and will not seem weird in any situation.

Choose any of the following items:

A HAT

Make sure that you select a good spy hat. This should be a hat you can easily tuck into your pocket, so you can put it on or take it off whenever you need to. Don't choose a hat that would be too eye-catching.

A good spy hat should be easy to pull down over your hair and eyes. It should be versatile, which means it should be one that you can wear in a variety of ways—like a wool hat that you can wear rolled up or rolled down.

SUNGLASSES

On a warm, sunny day, what could be more normal than wearing sunglasses? Slip on some shades to look instantly incognito. Not only will you disguise your identity, you'll also make it harder for other people to see exactly where you are looking, putting you at an advantage.

Spy Tip: Never use sunglasses as a disguise indoors, or during the winter—you are more likely to draw attention to yourself.

A SCARF

Keep a scarf in your bag to wrap around your neck at a moment's notice. A dark, plain scarf is better than brightly colored checks, for example. You don't want to stick out like a sore thumb!

LAYERS

Several thin layers of clothing, such as a couple of differently colored T-shirts, a thin sweater, a hooded top, and a light coat, give you lots of options for changing your appearance on a mission. Put whatever layers you are not wearing in a backpack, or change the order of the layers to create a completely different appearance.

REVERSIBLE CLOTHES

Keep a lookout for reversible clothing—for example, this could be a coat that is bright red, but when worn inside-out is dark blue. This is a supersimple way to change your identity. When spotted, just duck out of sight for a quick change and then disappear into the crowd.

HOW TO BUILD
A CAMOUFLAGED DEN

If you have a backyard or access to an outdoor space, why not build your own all-weather, camouflaged spying den?

You will need:

3 sturdy sticks, roughly 5 ft long
• 1 sturdy stick, roughly 6 1/2 ft long
• a ball of string • scissors • a large tarp or bedsheet
• some heavy stones • a small shovel

1. Decide where you want your den. Look for a sheltered area, out of the wind, and preferably on slightly raised ground for drainage. A good solid tree with a forked branch can form the back of your shelter, but a bush or wall works just as well.

2. Create a frame for your shelter by taking the three shorter sticks and tying them together about 6 inches from the top, with string, to form a tripod.

3. Place the final stick into the forks of the supporting sticks to form a ridge pole. Tie it securely with string. Rest the ridge pole in the branch of a tree, then push the supporting poles into the ground at a 45° angle. Check that these supports are firmly rooted in the ground. Alternatively, rest the ridge pole securely in a bush or on top of a wall.

4. Lay the sheet over the frame, leaving an opening at the front so that you can easily get in and out. There should be enough fabric to overlap at the front and keep out the wind.

5. Place the stones along the two ends of your sheet that touch the ground to weigh it down and keep it from blowing away in the wind.

6. Clear the ground inside your shelter so that it is comfortable to sit on.

7. Camouflage your den by plastering wet leaves, mud, light fallen branches, or grass over the sheet. This will also add an extra layer of insulation, making it warmer.

8. Use the shovel to dig a narrow trench around the sides and back of your den. This will channel rainwater away from the inside and help to keep you dry.

9. Furnish your den with cushions or camp chairs. Sit back and prepare for your first meeting.

HOW TO TEST A SPY'S MEMORY

Here are some tasks to help keep a recruit's memory sharp.

WHAT'S MISSING?

Place a dozen small items on a tray and give your recruit a minute to memorize them. Take the tray out of the room, remove three items, and move the remaining objects around. Return to the room and ask your spy to tell you which items are missing. Remove another three objects and ask your  recruit which objects are missing again. Do this once more so there are just three items left on the tray.

Mark the recruit's scores out of ten. Record the results using the chart template on page 127.

- Award one point for each item remembered.
- Give one bonus point if recruit remembers all nine removed objects.

SCENE IT

Sort through your photo albums, old postcards, or newspapers and magazines to find pictures of busy street scenes. Give your recruit one minute to study a scene. Now ask him five questions about the scene. For example:

"How many people are wearing hats?"
"What color was the car in the picture?"
"Was the person riding a bicycle male or female?"

31

You are testing his powers of recall and his ability to remember details. Mark your recruit's scores out of ten and record the results using the chart template on page 127.

- Give one point for each correct answer.
- Award a bonus point for extra detail on each answer.

IT'S ALL IN THE DETAILS

This final task will demonstrate a recruit's ability to remember details about people's appearances.

Show your recruit a photograph of a person randomly selected from a magazine. Give him one minute to study it, then hide the picture. Get your recruit to give you five clear, accurate details about the person in the picture. So, instead of, "He is medium height, medium brown hair, blue coat," look for interesting descriptions, such as, "He looked about 17, with short, dark curly hair, and a mole on his right cheek." This is just the kind of information that really helps to track the right people down and helps to avoid a mistaken identity.

Record your recruit's scores out of ten using the chart template on page 127.

- Give one point for each correct description.
- Award a bonus point for extra detail on each description.

TRAIN THE BRAIN

Don't give up if your potential recruit doesn't do well the first time. The brain is a muscle that gets stronger with practice. Repeat the tests and you should see an improvement in your recruit's scores. You'll soon have a team of super-agents!

HOW TO CREATE A BOOK SAFE

An old book is an excellent place to hide information or small pieces of spying equipment. You'll need a thick book with a hard cover to make a convincing "book safe." Your aim is to hollow out a rectangular compartment in the center of the book. If you don't have any books that you don't mind cutting up, visit a thrift store to find one.

You will need:

a thick, hardcover book, very studious-looking
• a sheet of cardboard • a pen • scissors
• a glue stick

1. Draw a rectangle on the sheet of cardboard that is 1 1/4 inches smaller on each side than the size of a page of your book. Cut the rectangle out to make a template. Now flip through the first 30 pages of your book.

2. Take the next five or six pages and fold them in half lengthwise, with the long edge pointing toward the center of the book as shown here.

3. Place your template in the center of the page and, with a thick pen, trace around its edge on the folded area of the page.

4. Cut around the outlined area on the folded pages with scissors. When you unfold the pages you should have a rectangular hole in the center.

5. Repeat steps 2 and 3, cutting five or six pages at a time, until you reach the last 30 pages of the book, which you should leave intact.

6. Cut four strips of cardboard that fit inside the four walls of your "safe." Cover them liberally with glue, then fit them in place to add extra strength to the hole.

7. Let your book safe dry.

Cover your tracks by cleaning up the equipment you used to make your safe.

Your book safe is now ready! Put coded notes and spy equipment inside and simply place it among other books on a shelf. To the casual observer, it should look just like any other "innocent" book.

HOW TO SHADOW A SUSPECT

Shadowing is one of the most important skills for a spy to master. Shadowing means that you can follow a target to find out just what they are up to, without ever being noticed.

SHADOWING SECRETS

Simple Disguise: Hide your identity—sunglasses to cover your eyes or a hat to conceal your hair will be fine. You'll need to dress in dark, muted colors, which means leave your favorite red shirt at home.

Supplies at the Ready: Carrying money at all times is essential in case your target gets aboard a bus or train. You wouldn't want to get left behind at the bus stop.

Target Identity: It may sound obvious, but make sure you're shadowing the right person—memorize their appearance that day. It would be embarrassing to realize you had shadowed the wrong person for several hours.

Keep Your Distance: Don't act as if you actually are your target's shadow—if they trip right over you, your presence will definitely be revealed. There's no need to get too close to your target. Try to stay on the opposite side of the street or a good distance behind.

Stop-Start Technique: If your target comes to a halt while walking, you should keep walking. Then find an opportunity to stop a little farther on. Try to vary your reason for stopping. You might be able to tie your laces once or twice without being noticed, but you will give yourself away if you do it more often. Pause to look in shop windows, ask someone for directions, or pause to check your phone for messages.

Watch without Looking: There are different ways to watch people without looking directly at them. Use shop windows, car windows, or mirrors to keep an eye on your target's movements. Practice sharpening your peripheral vision so that when you are looking straight ahead you can still watch your target out of the corner of your eye.

Keep Up: If your target seems to be getting too far ahead, don't walk faster or start to run—this will attract attention and risk blowing your cover. Instead, increase the length of your stride until you have caught up a little. If your target "vanishes" around a bend, simply sprint to reach the corner quickly. Just before you get to it, slow down to make sure you walk around the corner at your usual pace.

TEST YOUR TRAINING

Now that you know how to follow a target, it's time to put your shadowing skills to the test by practicing with a friend. Here's how:

1. Arrange to meet a friend somewhere busy—such as at a local store. Use the shadowing secrets from pages 35 and 36 to follow your target all the way from his house to the meeting point without being spotted. Don't be too ambitious—following a friend on his family vacation could be tricky.

2. Take a camera phone with you, if you have one, to detail his movements. Follow your target as he goes about his business. At various stages, pretend to make a phone call, but take photos or video footage of him instead. If you don't have a camera phone, use a small notebook and pen to record details of his movements.

3. Once your friend arrives at the prearranged location, innocently pretend to turn up for your meeting. Later, once your friend has returned home, show him the evidence of how well you tailed him throughout the day.

HOW TO THROW AN OPPONENT

Your mission has gone terribly wrong! Your identity has been discovered and an enemy agent is hot on your heels. He's getting closer, and even your best fake ID can't get you out of this. As your opponent approaches you from behind, you immediately realize that you're going to have to throw the enemy agent to make your escape. Here is a basic self-defense technique that will help you use your opponent's attack to your advantage.

WHAT TO DO

Spies have to be prepared for extreme situations, so practice this maneuver with a friend, taking turns being the attacker and defending yourself. Use a mat to soften your fall.

1. It's important to act quickly, so as soon as you feel your opponent's hand grab you, grip his arm firmly with both hands.

2. Rather than trying to pull his arm away from you, tug it forward and downward—this is much easier to do.

3. Take a big step forward, bringing your opponent with you. This will not only take him by surprise, but will also throw him off balance.

4. Without pausing, bend your knees into a crouching position and lean forward at the waist.

5. As your opponent begins falling forward, tilt your body to the side and use his momentum to pull him forward, landing him on his back on the mat.

Warning: Never practice this move on an unsuspecting opponent and always make sure that there are plenty of soft mats around to provide a soft landing while you are practicing.

Spy Tip: It is a great idea to learn this and other self-defense moves, so why not sign up for a real course run by an instructor?

HOW TO SET UP A FITNESS OBSTACLE COURSE

This simple obstacle course is guaranteed to keep you and your fellow agents in great shape. It is designed to test your speed, agility, stamina, and stealth over six obstacles. You'll need a few props, so prepare in advance to create the ultimate challenge.

You will need:

2 strong wooden planks • 8 bricks • a large tarp or an old bedsheet • 6 tires or hula hoops (or chalk to draw circles) • a collection of dry leaves and twigs or newspaper balls • a blindfold • 6 ordinary objects (such as a piece of fruit, a book, a shoe) • a backpack • a stopwatch or a watch with a second hand

Balance Beam: Set up one plank with a brick at either end to form a narrow balance beam. (If you have more planks, set them end to end to make the beam longer.) Carefully walk or run along the beam as quickly as possible. Agents must not fall off.

Commando Crawl: Clear an area the size of your tarp or sheet, removing any sharp twigs and stones. Lay the tarp on the ground and weigh down two opposite sides with three bricks each. (Don't stretch the tarp tight—you need enough slack in it for someone to squeeze underneath.)

Use your knees and elbows to crawl under the sheet "commando-style." Keep as low to the ground as you can. Agents must not knock any bricks off the tarp as they crawl under it.

Step-Up Sets: Use any step for this exercise, or set up your own step with a plank and bricks. To test fitness and stamina, step up and down ten times, alternating your feet for each step. Agents must complete the steps without pausing.

Stealthy Steps: Scatter your collection of leaves, twigs, or newspaper balls all over the ground, to cover an area roughly 6 1/2 square feet. Agents must be blindfolded, then attempt to get across the obstacle without any loud crunches.

Tire Out:
Place your tires or hula hoops on the ground in two staggered rows, or draw six circles on the ground in the same pattern. Jump through the tires as quickly as possible, alternating your feet and without stumbling.

Shuttle-Run Challenge: Place six objects in a line, roughly 6 1/2 feet apart and 30 feet from the open backpack. The mission, starting from the backpack, is to run back and forth, collecting one item at a time and packing them into the bag. Agents must carry the bag to the finish line at the end of the obstacle course. If any item is dropped, they lose the point available for this obstacle.

Spy Tip: As the agents improve, why not make things harder by telling them to go backward through the course, or to do some obstacles on one foot? If you have enough material, set up two sets of each obstacle so that agents can go head-to-head against each other.

Your obstacle course can be set up in any order you like as long as recruits know the correct route to take to the finish line. Time each attempt and record scores out of ten using the chart template on page 127. Watch how everyone improves with regular training.

- Give one point for each of the six obstacles completed without mistakes.
- Give one bonus point for completing any obstacle backward.
- Give one bonus point for completing any exercise on one foot.
- Give two bonus points to the person with the fastest time.

Try setting the course up differently each time to keep agents on their toes.

HOW TO HAVE
FUN WITH PHONETICS

In the phonetic alphabet each letter is assigned a specific word, so that it is impossible to mistake one letter for another in a radio or telephone conversation. You can use it to make sure your messages aren't misunderstood. Here's how:

PHONETIC ALPHABET

A:	Alfa	N:	November
B:	Bravo	O:	Oscar
C:	Charlie	P:	Papa
D:	Delta	Q:	Quebec
E:	Echo	R:	Romeo
F:	Foxtrot	S:	Sierra
G:	Golf	T:	Tango
H:	Hotel	U:	Uniform
I:	India	V:	Victor
J:	Juliet	W:	Winter
K:	Kilo	X:	X-Ray
L:	Lima	Y:	Yankee
M:	Mike	Z:	Zulu

Whenever you need to make sure a word or name is clear, simply use the list above to spell it out. You could even give yourselves your own "call signs"—perfect for when you want to be clear which person is speaking over a walkie-talkie.

Replace each of your initials with the phonetic alphabet words that represent them. So, if your name happened to be Simon Martin, your call sign would be "Sierra Mike."

HOW TO PLAN AN UNDERCOVER MISSION

Good planning is vital to the success of any mission, whether you're staging a rescue, on the lookout for enemy agents, or just staking out the local park. Here's how to make sure that every spy mission goes off without a hitch.

1. Create a "mission dossier"—a safe place to store and access all the information you need for each mission. This could be a folder on a computer or a paper document, but make sure it is well hidden and protected (see pages 20–21 and 81–83).

2. Make sure that all agents know exactly what the mission goal is and what you intend to do. Keep the details simple and clear. It should be something like "find enemy code wheel" (see pages 77–80 for how to make one).

3. Assign a clear task to each agent, so everyone knows exactly what is expected of him. In addition, each agent should know the tasks of all the other agents.

4. First perform a recon (short for reconnaissance mission). This means that you scout out the location of the mission in advance. Wear a disguise so that you aren't noticed, and take a camera if possible. Write down any obstacles, guards, or weak spots that might make your mission easier.

5. Prepare a back-up plan and rendezvous point in case something goes wrong.

6. Write everything listed opposite in your mission dossier— include photos and any relevant information from your recon. Then gather your fellow spies and discuss it all.

7. If there is time, have a practice run of the mission in advance. Check that the plan works well and that everyone knows what they are doing. If there isn't time for this, make sure you go over the plan with everyone thoroughly.

8. After the mission, gather your agents together and hold a debriefing (where everyone describes exactly what happened to them on the mission). Discuss what went right and what went wrong, so you learn from your experiences.

HOW TO SET UP A DEAD-LETTER DROP

A dead-letter drop can be a safe and discreet way for fellow spies to communicate without the risk of actually meeting in person. It should be located in a place where the message can be left for pickup by a fellow spy at a later time.

SECRETS FOR SUCCESS

When choosing a dead-letter drop, always keep in mind that the hiding place should be:

Inconspicuous: A park, street, or restaurant where there are lots of people are better places for dead-letter drops than an isolated area where you would easily be spotted.

Well-Hidden: You don't want innocent (or not-so-innocent) people to stumble across your message. Think about animals, too—a nosy bird or squirrel might eat or move your message if it is in an obvious spot.

Routine Routes: Think of a place near where you often walk—perhaps on the way to school or to the park. People may get suspicious if you have to think up a reason for going somewhere new each time you want to make a drop.

COVERT SUGGESTIONS

Stuck for ideas of where to make your first drop? Here are some more pointers:

Check Your Bearings: If there is a street sign at the end of your road, check to see how much room is behind it. Could you quickly tape a message there without prying eyes noticing? People won't look there except for your contact.

Rest Stop: Park benches are great places for dead-letter drops. What could be more natural than sitting down? While you're doing that, could you stick your message under the bench seat?

At the Movies: Plan well in advance to agree on the movie and on which seat you will use, then stick your message just under the right-hand armrest while you are watching the film. The darkness offers perfect cover for the drop and your contact can pick up the message at the next screening.

Nature Ramble: If you have a dog, taking it for a walk makes a great cover. Next time you're out with Rover, subtly scout around for a distinctive rock (large enough to conceal a message) or a hole in a tree.

Make sure the location works well for your contact, too.
Then, when you need to leave your message, stop to tie your
shoelace or pat your dog next to the rock or tree. While you're
doing that, drop off your secret message.

Two Spy Tips: Don't forget to protect your message from the
elements. Wrap it up in a plastic bag, so that it's watertight.
Make sure it is stuck down securely. It may be a while before
your contact can pick it up, and you don't want it to come
loose, which could lead to it being discovered.

Make a couple of test runs first, but leave meaningless
messages. Go back to check if they have been discovered or if
your contact has picked them up.

HOW TO DISGUISE YOUR MESSAGES

As soon as you write down secret information on paper your spy ring is vulnerable to infiltration (allowing sneaks and snoops to gain access to your group). This is why a wise spy goes to great lengths to disguise the secrets they are passing on by using codes and ciphers. Use these cryptic techniques to keep your secrets safe.

CODE ONE: SUBSTITUTION

The simplest way to encode your communications is to substitute each letter in your message for another. Here's how:

1. Write out the alphabet. Then write it out again underneath, but starting one place to the right—A below B, B below C, and so on, up to Z below A. This is your key.

2. Substitute the letter you want for the letter underneath and write out your coded message. So, "Come to HQ after school" becomes "Bnld sn GP zesdq rbgnnk."

3. Change your key regularly, varying the letter at which you start the substitute alphabet—it could be three or twenty places along. To show the decoder which letter you have substituted for A, make a tiny pinprick under that letter the first time it is used. For example, if you have substituted Z for A, as described above, make the pinprick under the first Z in the message.

4. When you have finished writing the coded message, destroy your key so it can't fall into enemy hands.

Spy Tip: Write your message out with spaces added randomly so that they do not correspond to the real breaks in the words. This will make the message even harder to figure out.

CODE TWO: SWITCH-UP

This code is based on switching and reswitching the letters in a message.

1. First, write out a message, such as:

"Meet at three in the park"

2. Now write the words in reverse order:

"park the in three at meet"

3. Then switch the first and last letter of each word:

"karp eht ni ehret ta teem"

4. Add two random letters, such as "ed" or "er" at the beginning or end of every other word to finish your cipher:

"Karped eht nied ehret taed teem"

Make sure that each member of your spy ring understands how to decipher this type of message.

CODE THREE: PIGPEN

This code is almost impossible to decipher unless you know the secret.

1. Draw two separate grids and write the alphabet in the grids, with two letters in each box of the grid—as shown opposite.

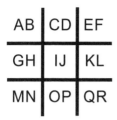 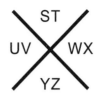

2. To write out the pigpen alphabet, the first letter in each box is shown with only the lines that surround it. The second is shown with the lines and a dot. "A" is shown as ⌋, "B" is ⌋, and so on. So, "Meet at three in the park" would look like this:

3. You can now assign a symbol to each letter using the section of its grid as a guide. Remember to add a dot to indicate when the letter is the second one within each box.

4. Make sure that all your agents know how you are writing out the alphabet and which grid you have put the letters into.

CODE FOUR: MADMEN

If you're ever pressed for time and have to whisper a message rather than write it down, it is still possible to encode it. Try this spoken code for a quick solution.

Add the word "mad" in front of the spoken vowels in each word. So a message such as "Help! Base is surrounded" becomes:

"Hmadelp! Bmadase madis smadurrmadomadundmaded"

CODE FIVE: TXT SPZ

If you have a cell phone, text messages are a great way to send coded messages that only you and your friends can understand. Make sure that you use as many abbreviations as possible and use initials that have secret meanings only you and your fellow spies know about. Most adults can't read text speak, anyway.

Here are a few suggestions to get you started:

- Replace the letter "L" with the number one
- Replace the letter "O" with the number zero
- Replace "to" with the number two
- Replace "for" with the number four
- Replace the plural ending "ies" with "Z"
- Replace double letters with a capital (for example, "soon" becomes sOn)
- Use "SYS" for "See You Soon"
- Use "9" for "Enemy Watching"
- Use "99" for "All Clear"
- Use "SOS" for "Spy Over Shoulder"
- Use "?" to say "I Have a Question"
- Use "!" to say "I Have a Comment"
- Use "MA" for "Mission Accomplished"
- Use "MAB" for "Meet At Base"
- Use "HOY" for "Help On Way"

Don't forget to delete your texts after you send or receive them so no one can read them on your phone.

HOW TO USE HAND SIGNALS WHILE ON OPERATION

Your mission has been a success. Your agents are within earshot of the enemy. It's vital that you give them instructions, but how? A walkie-talkie, even a whisper, could give away your positions. Here's your guide to some basic silent hand signals you need to know to communicate with your agents. Don't forget to practice so that your entire team knows what each gesture means and won't misunderstand an instruction.

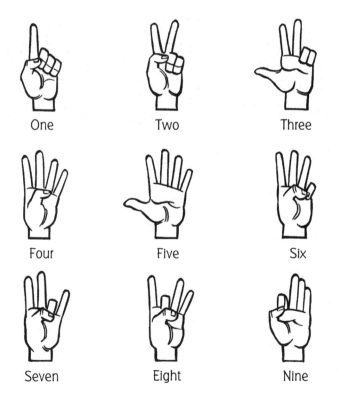

One   Two   Three

Four   Five   Six

Seven   Eight   Nine

Ten

You

Me

Come this way

Stop

Move faster

Walk in pairs

Single file

Get down

Understood/Okay

Not understood

Rendezvous

HOW TO BE THE BEST AT READING BODY LANGUAGE

Reading codes is one thing, but reading people's inner thoughts is much trickier. Does a smile mask an unpleasant intent? Should you trust that conversation or is the messenger leading you into a trap? Is that really an innocent passerby?

If you can decode body language, you'll be able to reveal someone's true feelings. So whenever you're talking to a contact or another spy, focus on his face and what he's doing. You may be surprised by what he's really thinking.

WARNING SIGNS

Look out for any of the following clues from people you talk to—these signs should send your spy antennae into overdrive:

• Do they raise their lip and wrinkle their nose? This means they find something you've said or something about you unpleasant.

• Do they smile for longer than a second, without the muscles around their eyes moving? This is a sure sign that the smile is fake.

• Are they picking at their clothes and/or looking at the floor? This can mean that they don't approve of your orders but aren't saying so. Defuse the situation by reassuring them and allowing them to discuss their concerns openly.

• Do they keep moving from one foot to the other? If they can't stand still or look directly at you, it's a sign that they are feeling guilty about something. Either that or they need to go to the bathroom!

• Do they keep rubbing at the back of their head? This can suggest impatience. Watch out for an emotional outburst—or try to calm them down and let them speak their mind first.

• Are they standing with their arms crossed? This is a sure sign that they are angry and ready for a fight. Stay calm, but don't let them out of your sight!

• Do they keep checking their hands or looking at the time? This means that they are bored. You'll need to make things a little more interesting if you're going to keep your spy ring going.

• If they narrow their eyes and tilt their head back, this is a real danger sign that someone doesn't like you. Watch out!

TELL A LIE FROM THE TRUTH

Most people find it impossible to control the things they do involuntarily when they tell a lie. There are lots of telltale signs that can give away double-crossing double agents. For example, you may notice their nose becomes redder or that their pupils dilate, becoming much larger than usual. Here are some other things that may signal they're not telling the truth:

> • Touching their nose a lot.
> • Refusing to make eye contact.
> • Sweating a lot.
> • Biting their nails.
> • Talking too much, with too much detail.
> • Making dramatic hand gestures.

If you're trying to give misleading information to a hostile agent, try to stop yourself from doing any of these things. Chances are the hostile agent may have been trained in reading body language, too.

Spy Tip: If you're with someone who sympathizes with you or believes in you, they will start to unconsciously mirror the gestures you make.

To test this, slowly cross one leg over the other and wait. The person you're with should mimic that move if they admire you. Keep your movements natural and try another gesture, such as leaning forward. Again, they should copy you.

HOW TO MAKE A SNOOPER PAPER

A newspaper is not only useful for keeping up with world events. A spy would also use one to shield his face from passing gazes and to blend into the background. This is even more effective with your own "Snooper Paper." Here's how to make one:

You will need:

a newspaper
- a sharp pencil
- a blob of sticky tack

1. Remove the front page of your newspaper (you'll need this later). Open the remaining paper at the middle pages and place it with the middle pages facedown on a table.

2. Place the blob of sticky tack under the first few pages of the paper, roughly 2 inches from the top and 2 inches from the center. Use the point of the pencil to pierce an eyehole through the pages all the way to the sticky tack, as shown.

3. Work through the rest of the newspaper in the same way, a few sheets at a time, creating an eyehole. Make sure the eyehole lines up through each layer.

4. Repeat on the opposite side to make the other eyehole—making sure the holes are the correct distance apart for you to see through.

5. On the front page of the newspaper, make two new eyeholes, 2 inches either side of the center, but this time, 2 1/2 inches from the top.

6. Test your Snooper Paper by lining up the layers. Slip the cover upward by 1/2 inch to line up the final layer. You'll be able to see through the eyeholes, but as soon as you lower the cover, the holes will disappear.

7. You're ready to take up position on a stakeout and use your Snooper Paper to track targets without being noticed. If you suspect anyone has noticed you, slip the cover down to block the eyeholes, roll up the paper, and walk away as casually as possible.

HOW TO GIVE YOUR AGENTS AN ACTION CHALLENGE

One of the most exciting things about being a spy is the unpredictable nature of the job. You never know what operation you might have to face, what could happen, and where you may end up. This means that the ability to improvise (which means thinking quickly and working with whatever is lying around) is a vital skill.

Gather the following items and test each of your agent's abilities to act under pressure. Some of the items are useful, but some are just decoys.

You will need:

a pair of nail scissors • an old pair of eyeglasses
• a paper clip • some mirrored cardboard • a tape measure
• a thin stick • a clear marble • a length of string
• adhesive tape • a ball of sticky tack • newspaper
• thick brown paper • shoe polish • a cell phone • a battery

Arrange the objects in front of your agent and describe the following scenario:

"You are outside a room in which a rival spy ring may be meeting. The door is slightly ajar, but you cannot tell who the people are.

"Your challenge is to use any of the objects in front of you to create a device that will enable you to get a glimpse inside the room. You must not enter the room."

Give him 15 minutes to try to figure something out, using only what is in front of him to come up with a solution.

What's the answer? There are actually at least two devices that can be made from these objects—both of them should help to solve the problem. Here's how:

MIRROR STICK

1. Attach the mirrored card to the end of the stick using the tape.

2. Add some weight to the opposite end of the stick, using the ball of sticky tack—this will give you better control.

3. Angle the mirror stick so that you can see through the open door into the room without being seen.

WIDE-ANGLE LENS

1. Roll the brown paper up into a long, thin tube.

2. Lodge the marble in one end of the paper tube so that it sticks halfway out.

3. Use the tape to keep the paper rolled securely and to stop the marble from rolling out.

4. Slowly push the completed device, marble-end first, into the room. Look through the opposite end. The marble will act as a wide-angle lens, enabling you to see all the way around the room (although it will be upside down).

Now that you know two possible answers, see how well your spies do and record their scores out of ten using the chart template on page 127.

- Give two points for finishing the task within 15 minutes.
- Give two bonus points if they finish in under five minutes.
- Give two points for demonstrating that their device works.
- Give two points if they work out the two different methods listed here within the time limit.
- Give two bonus points for a completely original method.

HELPING HAND

If your agents don't get anywhere near the answer, remove some of the decoy items to help them. If they still can't work out what to do, think about giving them a desk job instead!

HOW TO BECOME A REAL-LIFE SPY

To be a real spy, you'll need the eyesight of an eagle, the reflexes of an Olympic athlete, and the skills of a martial arts expert. Right? Not necessarily. Opportunities to become a spy can be open to ordinary people, too.

CRACK COMMUNICATOR

People who can translate conversations or documents from other languages are always needed. Do you speak another language?

TECHIE

If you're good with computers, you could find yourself tracking and tracing information, testing system security, and bugging important conversations.

LIFELONG LEADER

If you're a natural leader, you could find the perfect role running your own real-life spy ring and briefing agents.

ORGANIZED INTELLIGENCE

With so many agents in the field, spy rings need highly organized people to sort through all the information they receive. How organized are you?

HOW TO PURSUE A SUSPECT ON TOP OF A MOVING TRAIN

Imagine you are tailing a suspect and he takes off for Tibet on the Qingzang Railway — you'll obviously have to follow. When you're stuck on a train heading to Tibet it will be difficult to keep a low profile. If he notices you and tries to make a getaway you'll need to think fast to keep up, but would it ever really be possible to follow in the footsteps of James Bond and go after someone up top?

NECESSARY KNOW-HOW

Calling the guard or pulling the emergency cord might solve this problem without blowing your cover, but if you do find yourself on top of a moving train, here's how to follow:

1. Once you're up on the roof, kneel down and take a moment to get used to the motion of the train.

2. Don't try to stand up. Unless the train is moving at under 15 miles an hour, the wind resistance would knock you over.

3. Look in the direction the train is traveling before you start moving. Check for overhead hazards such as power cables, bridges, trees, or bushes.

4. Assuming the coast is clear, crawl along on all fours, or wriggle like a snake until you feel more confident.

5. If the train goes around a bend, lie flat and hang on to anything sticking up on the roof or "grab rails" on the side.

6. Crouch down, then move with the rhythm of the train

cars. This will mean moving in a zigzag pattern. Adopt a crablike or spiderlike gait, keeping your feet apart for balance.

7. Don't rush! Your suspect will not be moving any faster.

Warning: Never try this in the real world — not only would you be arrested, but it would be incredibly dangerous as well. Leave these antics in the safe hands of James Bond's stunt double.

HOW TO BECOME
A SURVEILLANCE EXPERT

When you're on a surveillance mission, vigilance is key. Have you ever thought that sometimes it would be useful to have eyes in the back of your head? A pocket "Sneakobook" is an easy way to give yourself exactly that advantage. Here's how to make one:

You will need:

2 small rectangular mirrors
• adhesive tape • white glue
• an old hardcover book you don't mind gluing

1. Place the two mirrors facedown on a flat surface. Line up the long edges, so that there is a narrow space between them, roughly 1/4 inch wide.

2. Place a strip of tape down the join. Add two or three extra strips for additional strength.

3. Turn over the mirrors. They should now be "hinged" by the tape. Check that they bend back and forth easily.

4. Open your book to the middle pages and place the mirrors in the middle of them. Make sure that the mirrors don't stick out beyond the edges of the pages.

5. When the mirrors are in a good position—the book should open and close easily—cover the back of the mirrors with glue, then shut the book, so they are glued into place. Let the glue dry.

6. Once the mirrors are firmly in place, open the book and pretend to read. You should be able to angle the book so that you can easily look in the mirrors to see behind you.

Spy Tip: On sunny days you need to be extremely careful to make sure the mirrors don't catch the sunlight and alert your "mark" (the subject under surveillance) to your presence.

HOW TO MAKE A CODE GRID

Code grids are an ingenious way to hide a secret message or communication within a seemingly innocent document.

You will need:

2 pieces of 8 1/2" x 11" cardstock (or thick paper)
• 8 1/2" x 11" sheet of graph paper
• 8 1/2" x 11" sheet of paper • a pencil • scissors
• some paper clips • a pin

1. Write down your secret message and count how many letters it contains. Let's say your message is "Meet me in ten minutes" — it contains 18 letters.

2. Use paper clips to fix the sheet of graph paper over the two pieces of cardstock, then shade in 18 squares (one square for each letter in your message) in random places on the graph paper. Use a pin to mark the corners of the 18 squares. Push hard enough for the pinpricks to penetrate both layers of cardstock.

3. Using the pinpricks to guide you, cut these squares out of both pieces of cardstock.

4. Unclip the cards and discard the graph paper.

5. Look closely at the pieces of card to make sure the holes are in identical positions. These are now your code grids. Pass one to your fellow agent and keep one for yourself.

6. Put one code grid over a blank sheet of paper and clip in place. Write your message in the holes — one letter per hole. Work left to right, going down the page as normal.

7. Fill the rest of the paper with other letters at random. You can even write whole sentences to make it appear just like any other innocent piece of paper.

8. Pass the message to your fellow agent.

9. The agent decoding the message just places his code grid over the piece of paper, revealing only the letters that make up your message in the pattern of the grid.

Spy Tip: Change grids regularly and build up a supply of them to use over time. That way, if one goes missing or falls into the wrong hands, you will still be able to safely communicate with your fellow spies.

HOW TO USE EMERGENCY SIGNALS

Codes are always an excellent way to communicate complicated messages, but sometimes something simpler and quicker will do. Here are a set of emergency signals your agents need to know about.

FACE SIGNALS

• Scratch your nose to signal "Danger, keep away."
• Brush your eyebrow to say "Let's rendezvous at base."
• Rub your right earlobe to signal "Follow me."
• Scratch your head to tell a fellow spy to follow the other person instead.

WINDOW SIGNALS

Place certain objects on the windowsill of your bedroom window to send clear messages to fellow spies.

• An empty drink bottle to say "The coast is clear, come on in."
• A backpack to alert everyone the spy HQ should be avoided.

- A picture frame to signal that everyone should meet at the usual place.
- The blind or curtain half drawn to say "Call off the plan."

PEN SIGNALS

Using a number of different colored pens, you can assign a code to each one to alert your fellow spies.

- Use a traffic light system—so that red means danger, green means all clear, and yellow means be careful. Put the pens into your shirt pocket with the colored caps showing.

- Agree to a simple set of signals with your fellow spies. For instance, the pen on the left could be the most important—the rest decoys. Your fellow spies will then be able to read the signal the pens make.

HOW TO MAKE A CAMOUFLAGE CARTON

It's easy to transform an innocent-looking juice carton into a safe place to store messages, codes, and other secrets of the spying trade!

You will need:

a one-liter juice carton
(drink the juice before you start)
• a dish cloth or paper towel
• scissors • adhesive tape

1. Clean the carton thoroughly before you get started.

2. Turn the empty carton on its side and grip firmly. Take the scissors and carefully pierce the carton at the top edge. You're aiming to cut around three sides only.

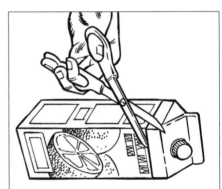

3. Leave one side uncut to act as a "hinge."

4. Flip open the top of the carton and make sure the insides are completely dry.

5. Apply tape all around the inside of the opening so that a small amount of tape sits just above the open edge as shown. The sticky side of the tape should face outward.

6. You can now stuff your camouflage carton with important papers and documents.

7. Carefully close the lid. Make sure the tape catches and makes a good seal.

8. Your camouflage carton is ready. Stash it out of sight in spy HQ—either at the back of a bookshelf or under the bed. This is good enough to fool most snoops.

Now not only will you have the perfect place to store important documents—you'll also impress people with how much juice you seem to drink!

HOW TO SIGNAL FROM A DISTANCE

Semaphore is a globally recognized way of signaling information. To be a semaphore signaler, all you need are two "flags" made from two differently colored triangles. Don't worry if you can't find actual semaphore flags—you can easily create your own. Here's how:

You will need:

2 squares of brightly colored fabric, 12 inches by 12 inches
• scissors • a needle and thread • 2 short sticks

1. Ask your parents for some old shirts or rags. Any fabric will do, as long as it's in bright, plain contrasting colors. You'll need enough for two squares.

2. Cut each square of fabric into two triangles. You should have four triangles in total—two of each color.

3. Sew the two contrasting triangles together along the diagonal line to create two flags using a simple backstitch.

4. Gather two short sticks from your yard.

5. Attach the sticks to one edge of the fabric by rolling the edge of your flag around the end of the stick and stitching along it. Make it a snug fit—you don't want your flag to slip when you are signaling. Sew up the top of the fabric so that the flag can't slip out of place.

6. Get plenty of practice extending your arms and holding the flags—semaphore can be a tiring business!

GETTING YOUR MESSAGE ACROSS

Once your flags are ready, you and your fellow spies need to learn the semaphore alphabet. There are several different positions for each arm: straight up, 45° down from vertical, straight out to the side, 45° down from horizontal, and straight down. To form some letters you will need to hold one arm across your body as well. The position of each arm can be combined to form a code that corresponds to numbers and to the letters of the alphabet.

SEMAPHORE SIGNALS

Here are the traditional semaphore signals for you to practice. If you need to get someone's attention with your flags, simply flap your arms up and down. If you make any mistakes, repeat the signal for the letter "E" (as in "error") five times. Then start over. Good luck.

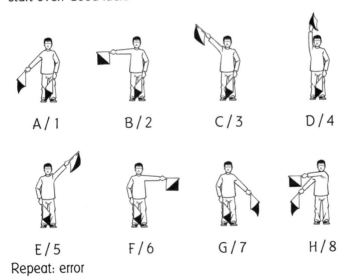

A / 1   B / 2   C / 3   D / 4

E / 5   F / 6   G / 7   H / 8
Repeat: error

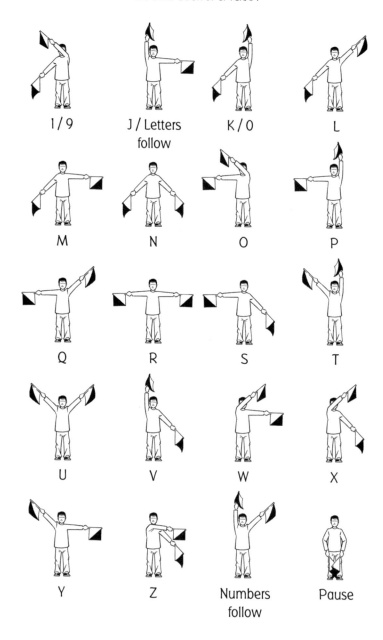

1 / 9

J / Letters follow

K / 0

L

M

N

O

P

Q

R

S

T

U

V

W

X

Y

Z

Numbers follow

Pause

HOW TO MAKE A CODE WHEEL

A code wheel is easy to make, and it creates a code that's almost uncrackable. You'll need to make two code wheels so that your message can be decoded by a fellow agent.

You will need:

- a brad paper fastener
- a sheet of thick 8 1/2" x 11" paper
- a pair of compasses
- scissors • a ruler • a pencil and pen • a protractor

1. Draw two circles onto your paper, 4 inches in diameter, using your compasses and a pencil. Cut them both out. Draw two inner rings onto one, from the same center point—one measuring 3 1/2 inches in diameter, the other measuring 2 1/2 inches in diameter.

2. Use your protractor to mark off 30 points around the edge of the smallest ring (each one will need to be at an angle of 12° from the next). Line your ruler up with the center of the circle and one of the points you have marked on the inner ring. Draw a line with your pen from this point to the edge of the circle. Repeat with each point around the edge, as shown on the template on page 79.

3. Write the letters of the alphabet, plus a period, an apostrophe, a question mark, and an exclamation point, around the outer ring, in a clockwise direction. Use the inner ring to write out the alphabet and punctuation marks again, this time in a counterclockwise direction, as shown on page 79.

Two Spy Tips: The positioning of the two alphabet rings determines your code. Start the inner alphabet ring where "T" appears on the outer ring, as shown, or pick another letter to make sure your code is different.

To be even sneakier, you could write out both alphabet circles randomly for an utterly uncrackable code.

4. Lay the second circle exactly over the other circle. Mark two windows on it, as shown in the diagram on page 80. One should line up over a letter in the outer alphabet ring and the other should line up over a letter in the inner ring.

5. Carefully cut out the two windows.

6. To join the two circles together, line up the centers with the alphabet circle at the bottom (there should still be marks from where you originally drew the circles). Make a hole with your pencil, then push the brad paper fastener through and split the ends to secure the two circles. The circles should rotate independently of each other.

7. Repeat steps 1 through 6 to make a duplicate code wheel. Hand this over to a fellow spy so he can decode your messages and send you messages of his own.

To use your coding device, spin the top wheel until it reveals the letter you need. Then look down to the notch on the opposite side and write down the letter displayed there. Continue until you have completely encoded your message.

CODE WHEEL TEMPLATE ONE

Shrewd spies can copy or trace over these templates and stick them onto circular pieces of cardstock to add extra strength.

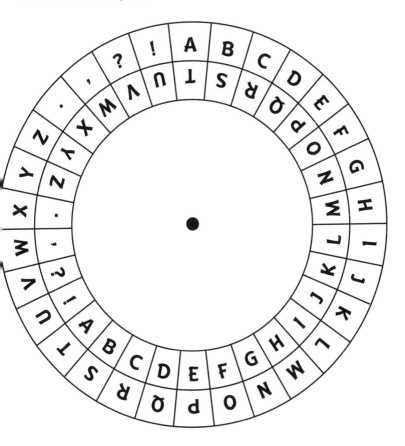

This is the template for the bottom half of your code wheel — the alphabet circle. Notice how the letters and punctuation run in opposite directions around the edge.

The template for the top circle is shown on the following page.

CODE WHEEL TEMPLATE TWO

This is the template for the top circle of your code wheel. You should turn the wheel to reveal the letter you wish to encrypt in the top window, then replace it with the letter shown in the bottom window.

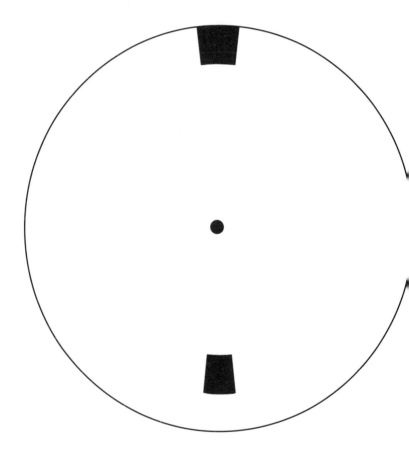

HOW TO HIDE FILES ON YOUR COMPUTER

If you have access to a computer, save time by using it to create spy documents. It's easy to store photos, add details of fellow spies, and report on any suspicious activities in a computer file. Unfortunately, it can also be easy for double agents to get all the information they need to break your spy ring wide open. It is essential to take a few basic precautions when using a computer.

1. Always bury your documents away inside one folder after another. At a minimum, your main spy folder should be hidden inside a folder, inside a folder, inside another folder—this adds three layers of security.

2. Name your spy folder something boring, but realistic, so there is no clue about its real contents. "Math Projects" should be enough to put off a casual browser. Use titles that relate to the folder name for documents saved within, such as "Math Homework This Month." Titles such as "Double Agents" or "Communication Codes" would immediately set off alarm bells.

3. Most computers display the most recent documents or folders that have been opened. A snooper is bound to check what you have been viewing. To divert attention, open a few random files or folders after you've been working on your spy folder—this will cover your tracks.

4. For extra security, add a password to your secret spy file. See pages 82-83 for password tips.

HOW TO CHOOSE
A GOOD PASSWORD

Disguising and burying top secret information on your computer should be enough to put most double agents off your trail, but there is an even better way to protect these documents: a well-chosen password.

The way that you set up password protection will be different depending on the program you use. As a guide, look for a "Security" or "Protect Document" heading, usually found within "Tools," and follow the instructions there. If you can't find the right section, use the "Help" function available with your software.

Once you've figured out how to set a password for a file, you'll need to choose a good one. Here are a few things you should (and shouldn't) do when creating a password:

DO

• Use a password that mixes numbers and letters, capital and lowercase letters.

• Choose a password that is at least six characters long.

• Avoid any word that you would find in a dictionary.

• Think of a memorable sentence. For instance: "My best friend is named Jack Hardy." Take the first letter of each word: m, b, f, i, n, j, h. Add in a capital letter and a number to replace a letter, such as the number one for the letter "i," for extra security and you have: "mBf1njh."

• Choose two short words that wouldn't usually go together, such as "bin" and "roof." Now add in some special characters again and you should come up with something like "b1Nr00f."

• Make sure that you don't use these examples!

DON'T

• Don't choose the word "password."

• Don't use any personal details—avoid your birthdate, your name, your pet's name, or the name of anyone else in your family.

• Don't write your password down anywhere.

• Don't give your password to anyone else.

• Don't keep using the same password—change it regularly.

HOW TO ENCODE E-MAILS QUICKLY

If you don't have time for a complex encryption, use this superspeedy method to send an ultra-urgent secret e-mail.

1. Type out your e-mail as quickly as you can—make sure that no one is looking over your shoulder as you write.

2. Before you send it, highlight all of the text and change the font from letters into symbols. Anyone who spots it will just see nonsense, but the recipient can simply switch the writing back to letters to read your message before quickly deleting it.

HOW TO MAKE YOUR ESCAPE

Even the most successful spies, like Alex Ryder and James Bond, can find themselves overwhelmed by enemy agents. Imagine you were captured by a rival organization and held against your will. How would you escape?

ESCAPE FROM BEING TIED UP

Tying you up would be a highly effective way of holding you prisoner, but only if you're tied up so well that you can't move.

Any knot can be untied if you can reach it with both hands. The most important thing for you to do while being tied up is to make sure that there is some slack or loose rope. Later on, this will enable you to move enough to reach the knots.

In order to do this, you need to work from the moment you are being tied up—every second counts. Bunch your fists and breathe in as much as possible to expand your muscles and your rib cage. Keep doing this until your rival spy has finished tying the last knot.

When you relax, you should find there is a fair amount of slack in the rope. Use the extra space you have to start loosening the knots.

ESCAPE FROM A PAIR OF HANDCUFFS

Handcuffs are impossible to open, right? Well, if you don't have any equipment, they are almost unbreakable. With the right tool, however, you can release them quite quickly. All you need is a simple, old-fashioned bobby pin. It is easy to hide one in the lining of a jacket or in a pocket, so make sure you have one within reach when you are captured. Try concealing it between your fingers or drop it on the floor within reach while you are being handcuffed. Then:

1. Once your captor has left the room, break the bobby pin so you can use the bendy section for grip and use the curved end for picking the lock.

2. Place the curved end into the keyhole on the cuffs, with the curve facing upward. Make sure it's in the flat part of the keyhole, parallel with the handcuffs.

3. Apply steady pressure and push the pin forward. The cuffs should spring open so that you can twist your hands out of them in one easy move.

ESCAPE FROM A LOCKED ROOM

Now that you're free from any handcuffs or ropes, how do you get past a locked door?

1. First, check to see if the key has been left in the lock. If it has, hunt around the room that you have been locked in for any useful equipment. Ideally, you'll be able to find a large sheet of paper and a pen or pencil.

2. Lay on the floor so that you can see though the gap between the door and the floor. Make sure that no one is around outside to see what you are up to. Keep an eye out for shadows approaching as you work.

3. Carefully and quietly, slide the piece of paper under the door, so that the largest portion of it is directly below the lock on the opposite side of the door.

4. Use the pen or pencil, or the bobby pin if you still have it, to gently push the key out of the lock from your side of the

door. As long as you don't push it too hard, the key should land on the piece of paper.

5. Slide the piece of paper slowly back toward you under the door, grab the key, and make your escape!

Warning: While it is fun to practice escape tactics with your friends, it is important to use common sense at all times. A true agent never plays practical jokes, such as leaving other agents tied up or locked in a room.

HOW TO WRITE IN INVISIBLE INK

Mastering the art of writing invisible messages is vital for any spy. It makes it easy to pass secret communications between one another, because if they fall into the wrong hands you don't need to panic. Double agents, traitors, or even parents won't realize what is going on. What's more, invisible writing is easy.

You will need:

a juicy lemon
• a calligraphy pen or thin paintbrush
• some paper • a heat source (such as a light bulb or a hair dryer)

1. Squeeze the juice out of the lemon and pick out the seeds.

2. Dip your writing implement into the juice and write your message or map onto the piece of paper. Write quickly, so that you can still see what you are writing before the juice dries.

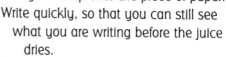

3. Wait for the "ink" to dry. As it does, your message should disappear.

4. Carrying or passing a blank piece of paper will raise suspicion, so you'll need to disguise the message.

You can do this easily by flipping over the piece of paper and writing a "normal" message on it. In addition, it's a good idea to sniff the message. If there's a telltale scent of lemon juice, borrow some cologne or aftershave and give the paper a quick spray to mask the smell.

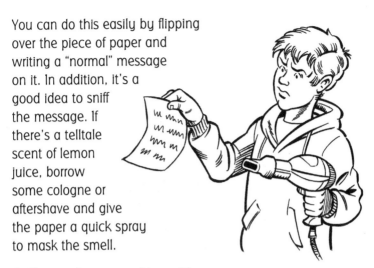

5. To reveal writing written with lemon juice, all you need to do is heat the paper. There are lots of ways you can do this—try using a hair dryer to blow hot air onto it or hold it close to a lightbulb. If neither of these work, ask an adult to put the paper on a tray in a hot oven or run a warm iron over the back of the piece of paper.

Warning: Always be careful not to set your message on fire by overheating it.

6. Destroy the message after reading it.

Spy Tip: Try apple juice instead of lemon juice. Use a toothpick to get juice from the apple and use it to write your message. Don't forget to eat the apple afterward to destroy the evidence. You could even use milk to write with if all else fails.

HOW TO SHAKE OFF A TAIL

In the shadowy world of international espionage, a successful spy is always alert and aware of the danger of being followed. A "tail" is a person who is secretly following you. Practice the following evasion tactics in your neighborhood with fellow trainee agents, so you'll always have the skills up your sleeve.

IN THE CITY

If your neck prickles and you get the feeling you're being followed, it's vital to identify your tail quickly. To take a look behind you without arousing suspicion, try one of these two tricks:

- Find a shop selling something you might be genuinely interested in (rather than a jewelry store, for example). Stop,

pretend to look at the window display, but then use the reflection in the glass to scan the street behind you.

• Stop at a parked car and pretend to check your hair in the window or side-view mirror. While you're checking out your look, check out the people around you, too.

GIVE THEM THE SLIP

It's easier to shake off a tail if plenty of other people are around to act as cover—so head for a busy area.

• Look for a crowd of people to mingle with—as soon as you reach a side street or store, slip out of sight.

• Stand casually by a bus stop. Once the bus pulls up, wait until the last possible moment to get on. Time it just right and you should be able to leave your tail in the dust.

- Casually and carefully cross to the opposite side of the street. When traffic blocks your shadow's view, duck down a side street and watch to see if your tactic has worked.

IN THE COUNTRY

It's harder to shake off a tail if you're in the country or a quiet area. There are fewer distractions to help you disappear, but it also means that your tail will have to keep their distance to avoid being spotted. Use this factor to your advantage and gain a head start.

- Dead twigs and leaves can be a dead giveaway as you rustle through them. If you must walk across dry forest terrain, check where you step to avoid making too much noise. Walking backward, sweeping leaves after each step to cover your tracks, may help to confuse your tail.

- Use muddy or sandy terrain to your advantage by setting a false trail. Leave clear tracks until you reach solid ground, then walk backward in your original footprints before taking a different direction, covering your steps behind you.

- If you come across a shallow stream, this is an ideal opportunity to lose your tail. Simply walk in the streambed for several feet before continuing on your way—your tail should not be able to see where the trail continues and will fall behind. Although you will end up with wet feet, it will be worth it in the end.

Warning: Always make sure that a stream is shallow with slow running water so that it is safe enough to walk in. You don't want it to sweep you off your feet, so be careful.

HOW TO MAKE A SECRET MESSAGE MARKER

Imagine the situation: You've been caught by an enemy agent who is searching you for secret messages. They find some strips of scrap paper, a pencil, and a marker in your pockets and snarl in disappointment. There's obviously been a mistake—you're just an innocent civilian . . . or are you?

Well, no actually. The enemy agent obviously hasn't heard of a "scytale"—an ingenious way to write secret messages without raising suspicions.

You will need:

an 8 1/2" x 11" sheet of plain paper
• a ruler • scissors • a thick marker
• adhesive tape • a pencil or pen

1. Mark off a narrow strip 1/4 inch wide along the length of the paper using your ruler and pencil. Carefully cut along the marked line so you have an even strip of paper.

2. Tape one end to the marker and wrap the strip around it in a spiral. Make sure that the edges of the paper meet but do not overlap.

3. Use another piece of tape to secure the other end.

4. Lay the marker on a desk or other flat surface.

5. Take your pencil or pen and write your message on the paper along the length of the marker. You'll need to keep your message short, but once you reach the end of the marker, you can turn it until the paper is clear and then write along it again.

6. Carefully undo the tape at either end. Then unwind the strip of paper and smooth it out.

7. Holding the piece of paper flat, the message you have written should look like a jumble of nonsense scribbles.

8. To decipher the message, all that a friendly spy needs is a marker of the same thickness that they can wind the paper around. This will reveal the secret message.

HOW TO BE A MASTER OF DISGUISE

If you're trying to tail somebody who knows what you look like, you'll need to work much harder than usual to hide your true identity. Try a combination of these great disguise tips to create a whole new you (see pages 27 and 28 for some quick-fix disguises for when you're in a hurry).

- To make you look older and conceal your features, add some subtle facial hair. Keep it simple though—prepare a pair of sideburns from cotton wool glued onto pieces of cardstock rather than trying to make a whole fake beard.

- Make yourself look larger by wearing lots of additional layers. Tie a pillow around your waist and add a thick coat to cover it.

- Add instant gray by dusting your hair and eyebrows with talcum powder.

- Fold several newspaper sheets into wedges. Put them in the heels or the toes of your shoes to alter your center of balance. You will tilt forward or backward, changing the way you move your arms and hold your head as you walk.

QUICK-FIX WRINKLES

A great way to make yourself look older is by faking some wrinkles. Here's how to create the perfect look:

You will need:

flesh-colored face paint or foundation makeup
- pink or red face paint or lipstick
- dark brown face paint or dark eyeliner pencil
- white face paint or white eyeliner pencil
- a thin paintbrush

1. Blend a little foundation or flesh-colored face paint over your lips to cover them. Then repaint your lips to appear slightly thinner using the red or pink face paint or lipstick.

2. Use the dark pencil or paint to draw a series of narrow vertical lines above your top lip and down into the corners of your mouth where creases form. Make sure you don't overdo the lines — experiment in front of a mirror until they look convincing.

3. Wrinkle up your forehead and scrunch up your eyes to see where your face creases naturally. Again use the dark pencil or paint to draw thin lines that follow the natural creases. This will exaggerate them.

4. With a clean finger, gently blend the edges of the wrinkles you have drawn into your skin.

5. Using the white face paint, draw a thin line on either side of each wrinkle and blend with a clean finger again. This will give a more convincing three-dimensional effect.

HOW TO WRITE INVISIBLE MESSAGES

Spies always need to improvise, and, if you need to write a secret message in a hurry, don't worry. There's more than one way to put pen to paper privately.

WAXING LYRICAL

1. Have a look around your house for candles. Look for ones that match the color of the paper you're writing your message on—if you have white paper, you need a white candle.

2. If the candle is new, it will already have a pointed end. Just cut off the wick before you get started. If the candle has been used, cut off the top and sharpen it so that you have a good writing point to use like a pen.

3. Write a decoy message in pen on one side to disguise your secret message. Turn the paper over and write your message using the candle—press firmly to leave enough wax behind.

4. To reveal the secret message, sprinkle pencil shavings across the paper, which will stick to the wax, or use a dark crayon to scribble over the piece of paper. The waxy writing will then mysteriously appear.

HARD-PRESSED

1. Write a message on a pad of paper using a ballpoint pen. Press down hard on the top sheet of paper.

2. Remove the sheet you wrote on and destroy it.

3. The sheet below will contain your hidden message. To a casual observer, it should appear blank, but if a fellow agent gently scribbles over it with a pencil, the message will be revealed.

NEAT AS A PIN

There is a great way to send a message without writing anything at all. Intrigued? Here's how to do it:

1. Find a newspaper and a pin. Open the paper at a random page that has lots of text on it.

2. Working across the page from left to right, make tiny pinpricks under each letter in the paper, spelling out the words in the order that they appear in your message.

3. Fold the corner of the page down to mark it. Close the paper, then transfer it to a fellow spy using a dead-letter drop (see pages 46–48).

4. If intercepted, the newspaper will look perfectly normal to an enemy agent. The person that wants to read the message simply needs to hold the correct page up to a light to reveal which letters have holes beneath them.

5. The page must be destroyed immediately after decoding the message.

WETTER IS BETTER

1. Grab two pieces of paper and a bowl of cold water. Dip one sheet quickly into the water, remove it, and lay it flat.

2. Lay the second, dry piece of paper over the wet one.

3. Use a pen or pencil to write your message on the dry top sheet. Press as hard as you can without ripping the wet lower sheet. Then destroy the top sheet.

4. At first you will be able to see your message on the damp sheet quite easily—don't worry, though.

5. Hang the wet paper to dry. Or, give it a quick blast with a hair dryer.

6. Once dry, pass the message to a fellow agent.

7. To reveal the hidden writing, all your fellow spies need to do is to get the paper wet again!

HOW TO PARACHUTE INTO ENEMY TERRITORY

Imagine flying deep into enemy territory on a clear, starlit evening. Your plane keeps low to avoid radar detection, skimming above the hills and trees below. This will be a "LALO" (Low Altitude, Low Opening) parachute jump. Give a confident thumbs-up to your fellow spy when the pilot signals it's time for the drop. Then get ready to exit the plane!

Here's what you need to remember to ensure success:

1. Push yourself out of the plane, holding your body in the arc position — chest first. Make sure you get well away from the plane, and that you don't fall over.

2. As you fall through the air, take a deep breath and, with your eyes on the horizon, count slowly to four before pulling the cord. Once the familiar, bone-jarring sensation of the parachute opening occurs, look up to check that the lines and parachute canopy are not tangled. If anything is wrong, quickly pull the cutaway cord and then the reserve cord — at low altitude, there's no time to lose.

3. You're the first one out of the plane, so you should have a clear route to the ground. Locate your fellow jumper and stay alert at all times to avoid a collision. Steer yourself toward the landing zone, using the left and right steering lines, and looking before each turn.

4. Prepare for landing. As the ground gets closer, turn your body into the wind for the final turn. This will slow your descent as much as possible and ensure you're in control of your parachute. As agreed in the mission plan, both of you should make this last turn to the right, so that you don't crash into each other. Use your right-hand steering line to guide you, making adjustments with the left.

5. Pull on both steering lines at once to flare the canopy and slow your descent. As the ground rushes toward you, move your body into an arc. As soon as the balls of your feet hit the ground, you should continue falling in the direction your parachute drifts. Rest your chin on your chest and twist with your hips. This will cushion your fall as your legs give way on impact with the ground.

6. Wait for a second as the air rushes back into your lungs, then gather your thoughts. You have to get to your feet quickly and check that all is well — no injuries or breaks and no signs that you've been spotted.

7. Before there's time for anyone to raise the alarm you need to look around to spot where your fellow spy is landing, then start gathering your parachute. Stash the 'chute in some bushes, then make for the rendezvous point. And always stick to the plan.

HOW TO BE A MORSE MASTER

Morse code has been around for over 150 years. It was originally invented by Samuel F. B. Morse in the United States and was used for military communications and radiotelegraphy. It is one of the simplest and most versatile codes around, and it's a great way for you and your fellow spies to communicate. This code can be written out, tapped out, or even flashed using flashlights.

The different combinations of dots, "·," or "dits," and dashes, "-," or "dahs," are used to represent each letter of the alphabet. A

"···/·/· ·---/---/··- ·---/·-/-/·/·-
··-/·---/·---/··/---/·-/-/---/·-··"

dit should last the length of time it takes to say the word "dit." A dah should last three times longer than a dit.

The secret to mastering Morse is to get comfortable with the difference in timing between a dit, a dah, and a break between words.

Once you've mastered the timing, you'll need to learn the Morse code alphabet, shown opposite.

Translation: see you later alligator

MORSE CODE ALPHABET AND NUMBERS

A:	·-	**M:**	--	**Y:**	-·--
B:	-···	**N:**	-·	**Z:**	--··
C:	-·-·	**O:**	---	**1:**	·----
D:	-··	**P:**	·--·	**2:**	··---
E:	·	**Q:**	--·-	**3:**	···--
F:	··-·	**R:**	·-·	**4:**	····-
G:	--·	**S:**	···	**5:**	·····
H:	····	**T:**	-	**6:**	-····
I:	··	**U:**	··-	**7:**	--···
J:	·---	**V:**	···-	**8:**	---··
K:	-·-	**W:**	·--	**9:**	----·
L:	·-··	**X:**	-··-	**0:**	-----

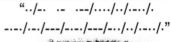

"··/-· ·- ·--/····/··/·-··/·
-·-·/·-·/---/-·-·/---/-·/··/·-··/·."

To leave a break between words, say "dit" to yourself five times. This will allow a long enough pause before you start the next word in your sentence.

Start off slowly at first — you'll be able to build up more speed the better you get.

Can you translate the message above each picture? Slashes have been used to clearly separate individual letters.

Translation: in a while crocodile

HOW TO CREATE A FAKE ID

You're on a top secret mission and you need to gain access to a certain mysterious-looking building. When two suspicious guards stop you, how will you manage to get past?

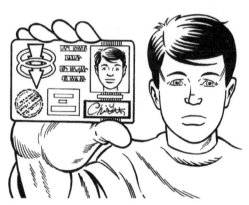

Simple—your own identity card. Here's how you can make an ID card to suit any mission you might undertake.

You will need:

a passport photo of yourself (possibly
in the disguise you're going to wear)
• a thin sheet of plain, white cardstock
• scissors • a computer (or a pen)
• some ink (preferably in a stamp pad)
• a potato (yes, a potato)
• a small kitchen knife • a pencil
• sticky-backed plastic

1. Carefully cut a piece of paper to the size of a standard debit or credit card (ask to borrow one of your parents' cards to get the measurements).

2. Stick your photo in the top right-hand corner of the credit card–sized paper.

3. Now add details around your fake ID picture. You can do this with a pen if you're careful or on a computer for a more professional finish. Include a fake name, a fake ID number, a fake phone number, and the "department" you work for.

4. At the top of the card, include your fake employer's name. If you're using a computer, design your own company logo and paste it onto your ID card. Why not pretend you're from a water or electricity company to give yourself a realistic but vague excuse for being there?

5. Add a signature at the bottom of your fake ID—the less readable it is, the better. Remember to sign your fake name!

6. Now you need to add an official-looking stamp in the bottom corner of the card. To do this, carefully cut the potato in half with the knife. Dab the cut end with a paper towel to soak up the juice. Now draw on a simple design using your pencil. Carefully use the knife to cut out the background, leaving your design standing proud. Dip the potato into the ink. Make sure the design is covered.

7. Firmly stamp the potato print onto your ID card. Once the ink is dry, cover the front and back of the card in sticky-backed plastic to give it a glossy finish.

Spy Tip: If you have access to a computer, the perfect ID card will be even simpler to make. Work on your designs and build up a whole library of fake ID cards. You can prepare a new one before every mission!

HOW TO MAKE A SECRET MESSAGE SQUARE

Secret message squares offer a great way to communicate with other spies. They're small, so they're easy to conceal in the palm of your hand. They're hard to open, giving you extra security. They're sturdy, so you can throw them or even get them damp without spoiling the contents.

You will need:

several sheets of plain paper
• a pencil and ruler • scissors

1. Your message squares need to be small enough to hide, so carefully cut your paper to size in advance—4 inches by 5 inches.

2. Write your coded message on one side of the paper.

3. Fold the paper in half lengthwise, with the writing on the inside. Then fold it lengthwise again. Your message should now be safely hidden inside the narrow strip of paper you are holding.

4. Lay the strip on a flat surface. Fold the top right-hand corner over into a triangle and the bottom left-hand corner up into a triangle, as shown below:

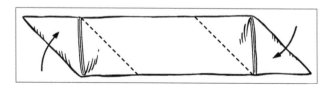

5. Fold the triangles inward along the dotted lines as shown in the previous picture. You should now have a shape that looks like a lightning bolt, with a diamond shape at either end and a square in the center.

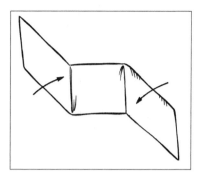

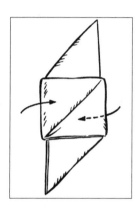

6. Take one diamond shape and fold it across the front of the central square. Then fold the other diamond shape across the back of the central square in the opposite direction as shown.

7. You now need to tuck the two remaining triangles inside. Fold the first one underneath the central triangle. Then turn the square upside down and repeat on the opposite side. Press firmly to secure.

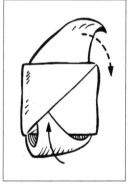

Spy Tip: This technique gets easier with practice. Try to make the creases as clean as possible by using the ruler to create sharp, straight edges that you can fold the paper over.

HOW TO CREATE SECRET SIGNALS AND SIGNPOSTS

If you're following a suspect and can't call for help, it's easy to leave a secret trail behind for your fellow agents to follow. Here are a few simple precautions to bear in mind:

- Plan a series of signs in advance to make sure that your fellow agents know what your signs mean (see opposite).

- Use natural objects that you can find lying around, or use chalk to write signs that can easily be removed.

- Don't destroy or permanently mark any objects when you leave your trail.

- Don't overuse signs—the more signs you leave, the more likely they are to be spotted. Only leave a sign if you have something important to point out.

- Place signs near the route but not on a path where they might be disturbed or destroyed.

- If you're following a trail of signposts, always erase or rearrange them as you move on so that no one else can follow them.

SECRET SIGNS

The signs you leave don't need to be complicated. They should be easy to leave, easy to remove, and easy to understand. Here are some classic signs to get you started:

TRAIL SIGNS AND THEIR MEANINGS

An arrow made from twigs:
This way

A small stone in the middle of
a larger stone:
You're on the right trail

A small stone to the left of a
larger stone: Turn left

A small stone to the right of a
larger stone: Turn right

A circle of stones around a
central stone:
Gone home / cancel trail

A circle of stones around a
number of pebbles: shows number of
paces you should walk in direction of
arrow to find a message

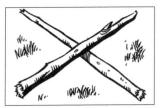

A cross made of twigs:
Don't go this way

A triangle made of twigs:
Warning

HOW TO SEE EVERYTHING WITHOUT BEING SPOTTED

Get the best view of any suspicious activities, even if you're behind a wall or around a corner, with your very own spy periscope. Here's how to make one:

You will need:

2 cardboard juice cartons
• a marker • scissors • a ruler • strong tape
• 2 flat mirrors or mirrored cardstock
• poster paints—various colors

1. Carefully use the scissors to cut out a square opening at the bottom of one carton as shown. Leave a half inch frame around the sides and bottom of the opening for strength.

2. Place the carton on its side with the square opening toward you. Use your ruler to draw a diagonal line at a 45° angle, from the corner nearest the opening, as shown here.

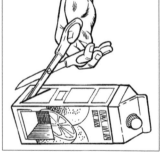

3. Carefully cut along the line you have drawn. Slide the mirror into this slot. Check that you can see the top of the carton reflected in the mirror through the hole you've already made in the front. Then use the strong tape to fix the mirror in place.

4. Repeat steps 1 through 3 with the other carton.

5. Carefully remove the roof-shaped tops from each carton with the scissors.

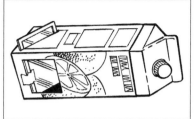

6. Position the cartons with their open ends together, with one mirror facing you and the other mirror facing in the opposite direction. Look at the mirror facing you. You should see the view from the other mirror reflected into it. Use the strong tape to join the cartons together.

7. Cover the juice cartons in poster paints to disguise them. You could use brown and green paints for a forest stakeout, sandy colors for desert reconnaissance, or shades of white and gray for surveillance in snowy conditions.

Your periscope is complete! Take it for a test run. Use it upright to find out what's going on over a wall, or use it on its side to find out who is coming around a corner.

HOW TO MAKE A SPY RING BUTTON

Buttons are an essential part of a spy's equipment—they can be worn as subtle signals to other spies, with different buttons having different meanings. You and your fellow agents should buy or make a number of buttons with the same designs, so that each spy has a matching set.

Your set should include: one red, one green, one blue, one yellow, one with a star, and one with an x on it. You can get button-making kits from craft shops and there are even websites where you can order your own button designs.

WHAT TO DO

1. In advance, you should all agree what each button design means.

For example, you could use:

- a red button to signal danger

- a green one to signal that all is clear

- a yellow one to signal that the spy ring needs to meet at base soon

- a blue button to signal that you have a message to deliver

2. Start by wearing the x button regularly, so people are used to you wearing a button, and you don't arouse suspicions. The x means that there is no message.

3. Choose the star button as an "identifier"—a secret way of identifying yourself as a member of the spy ring. This also enables you to spot other friendly spies without having to make contact with them.

4. When you need to send a signal, just pin on the most appropriate button during your next mission.

Spy Tip: Use a button to carry secret messages—if you're in a hurry, buttons can be used to hide messages that you don't want enemy agents to see. Fold the message up very small and wedge it in the back of the button. For extra security, use a small amount of tape to keep it in place or pierce it with the button pin. Pin the button to your clothes as usual—no one will suspect you are carrying a secret message!

HOW TO COMPLETE AN UNDERSEA RESCUE

You're on a mission to infiltrate the underwater HQ of an international criminal mastermind. You and your fellow agent must scuba dive through the secret underwater entrance to the cave in order to take the enemy by surprise.

Once you have safety-checked your diving gear and put it on, fall back into the warm sea, holding your mask and snorkel to your face. Wait for the cloud of bubbles to clear. Give your fellow agent the "okay" signal (see page 54) and kick down to the reef. A school of fish flashes silver as you swim past. You spot the entrance to the cave less than 150 feet away.

Suddenly, you realize that your companion has stopped swimming. He's waving frantically at you—something has gone wrong and he's suddenly out of air! You'll need to share your air supply. Here's what to do:

1. Swim over to your partner and hold onto his jacket with your left hand.

2. Take a deep breath and then calmly remove the regulator (mouthpiece) from your mouth.

3. Push the button on the regulator to clear it of water and then hand it to your fellow agent. Hold up three fingers to tell him to take three breaths.

4. When he has finished and hands back the regulator, clear it again as you did before. Do this at every exchange.

5. Continue to hold onto each other and breathe in

this way until you have established a rhythm and your companion has calmed down.

6. When you are both ready, give a thumbs-up to signal you are heading back up to the surface. Lead the ascent and swim upward at a steady rate—at a speed no faster than your bubbles.

7. When you break the surface, head straight back to the support boat. Report to base and return to the safe house on shore. Your mission has just been postponed.

Warning: Before attempting any kind of a scuba-diving rescue in the real world, seek training with a qualified instructor—or you may find you need rescuing yourself.

HOW TO USE A WALKIE-TALKIE

If you're lucky enough to have a walkie-talkie set, you'll know what a great piece of equipment it is, making it easier for you to stay in touch whenever you're on a mission.

It's also very easy for anyone nearby to listen in and overhear

what you're saying, though . . . unless you can confuse communications with the "10" code system.

Police forces use "10" codes to keep conversations over the radio as short as possible. You can use the same system, or develop your own version, so that only you and your fellow agents know what you are talking about.

SOME STARTERS FOR "TEN"

Here are some useful phrases from *The Boys' Book of Spycraft* version of the "10"-code system to get you started. Get together with everyone in your spy ring and memorize this code:

- "10–1" means "I can't hear you"
- "10–2" means "I can hear you loud and clear"
- "10–3" means "stop speaking"
- "10–4" means "message understood"
- "10–5 *[plus name]*" means "pass message to *[plus name]*"

- "10-6" means "please repeat what you said"
- "10-7" means "no"
- "10-8" means "stand by for a message"
- "10-9" means "other people are present and listening"
- "10-10" means "urgent, help needed"
- "10-11" means "return to base"
- "10-12" means "where are you?"
- "10-12 *[plus location]*" means "I am in *[plus location]*"
- "10-13" means "abandon operation"
- "10-14" means "false alarm" or "all clear"

ROGER, ROGER?

To sound like a professional radio operator, you'll need to use proper "voice procedure." Here's what you should say and when to say it:

- "Roger" for "message received"
- "Copy" for "message is understood"
- "Wilco" for "will comply" — you're going to follow the instructions
- "Say again" for "repeat message"
- "Over" to say "my message is complete, waiting for a response"
- "Out" to say that the conversation is complete

Spy Tip: Use the sound of your voice to indicate whether or not you are asking a question or making a statement. For example, if you say "copy," it sounds as though you have understood the other agent's message. If you say "copy?" he will know that you are asking if he has understood your message.

HOW TO USE A CODEBOOK

Books aren't just useful for concealing equipment (see pages 33–34) or for hiding mirrors on surveillance missions (see pages 66–67). They can also be used to create a highly secure code.

Here's how:

1. All the spies in your ring need to get exactly the same edition of a book. You can choose any book you want, although it's a good idea to use one that is quite long (between two and three hundred pages) so that it has plenty of words in it. This will be your codebook.

2. When writing a secret message to your fellow spies you'll need to identify the page number, the line number, and the number of words along the line that each word appears. Everyone should agree in which order you will encode these to pinpoint specific words in the book, such as "page — line — word."

For example, if the first word in your coded message is "meet," flip through your codebook until you find this word in it. If the word "meet" appears on page 12, that will be the first part of your code: "12." Then to narrow down the search for this word, identify which line the word is on. Count down from the top of the page. If "meet" is on line 15 of page 12, your code would read: "12 — 15." The final piece of information your fellow spies need is how far along that line to look. Assuming that "meet" is the third word along from the left, you should then add this number to the code you have already written: "12 — 15 — 3."

Must cancel meeting—I have to go to my sister's ballet recital. J.

3. Write out the code for each word of your message in a column of numbers. Only your fellow spies, who know exactly which book to use to decode it, will understand what you have written.

You can receive similarly encoded messages in return. As long as the identity of your codebook remains secret, it will be almost impossible for anyone else to crack your code and decipher your communications.

117—27—5? (Use this book to decode that message!)

HOW TO CRACK A CODE

Once you have learned how to make all the codes in this book, you will be one step closer to knowing how to crack any coded messages you might intercept from rival agents. A substitution code (see page 49) is the easiest to practice breaking. To help you out, here are some tricks to try to become a killer code-cracker.

1. Look for any repeated letters or sequences of letters. Any recurring pattern will help you identify the type of code used.

2. Try swapping the first and last letters of words in the code in case any obvious solutions jump out at you.

3. Check what happens if you write the message out backward—you may see some words you recognize.

4. Look out for the most common symbol or letter that appears in the message. In the English language the most common letter is "E," so that letter in your message is almost certainly an "E." Try to work out if there is a pattern between the code version of "E" and the letter "E." For example, if the letter "E" appears as an "F" every time in the message, it would suggest that code has been made by replacing each letter with the one next to it in the alphabet.

5. As soon as you find a letter you have decoded, write it in capitals under the symbol or coded letter.

6. Look out for any short words that could be "to," "and," "at," "I," or "a." The most common three-letter word in English is "the." If you recognize an "E" at the end of a three-letter word, write "T" and "H" below the corresponding letters.

7. Slowly build up the number of letters you think you can decode. Once you have two or three, you may be able to start guessing at more words. If you have decoded two letters on either side of one another, take an educated guess at what it might be. Then see what happens if you write the decoded letter under the coded version in other places.

8. Look for patterns in words. If you decode a "Q," the next letter is most likely a "U." "H" often follows "C" and so on.

9. Don't be afraid to experiment and get things wrong, but as soon as you decode a letter, keep thinking about how it could unlock the entire code.

10. Don't give up! Once you figure out two or three letters, you should have enough to crack any substitution code.

DECRYPTION TEST

Write out a copy of these coded messages for each of your recruits. Get them to try out their code-breaking skills using the methods described here. Give two points for each code they break, one point if they need a clue, and none if they flunk out completely. Clues and solutions are on page 125. Record their results using the chart template on page 127.

1. Qeb pmv jxpqbo fp lrqpqxkafkd.
2. Ztte je iwt vdds ldgz, ndj'gt vtiixcv qtiitg paa iwt ixbt.
3. Svzwjfzigvih szh yvvm rmezwvw—wl mlg zkkilzxs.
4. Rednfiltratei neeber sahed ginred reyps ruore.
5. Maxx buva, kuo era vum e weqpar cuba-draeyar.

HOW TO MAKE A FOOLPROOF DISGUISE

When it comes to disguises, it's tempting to create one that will let you blend into the background so you are *not* noticed. However, you can take the opposite approach and stand out from the crowd. Disguising yourself as a victim of an accident will give you an unthreatening appearance—no one will imagine that you're a highly-trained spy.

You will need:

black tooth enamel, available from joke stores
• cotton balls and small sponges • makeup/face paints in black, red, purple, green, yellow, and blue
• a couple of thin paintbrushes • a large fabric square or a dish towel • a safety pin • a small stone

A MISSING TOOTH

1. Use a cotton ball to dry the tooth you are going to pretend is missing.

2. Paint the black tooth enamel over the tooth, covering it completely. From a distance there will appear to be a gap where your tooth used to be.

3. Hold your lip up until the enamel dries. The enamel will rub off easily when you want to remove your disguise.

A SPLIT LIP

1. Dip your brush into the red makeup and draw it over your top lip and up toward your nose in a thin line.

2. Make the red "cut" wider at the bottom, to give the effect that the skin is split.

3. Using clean brushes, apply some yellow and purple makeup to each edge of your cut to make it look puffier.

4. Carefully add a narrow line of black down the center of your cut, so it looks deep.

5. Use a piece of cotton wool to blend the "bruising" around the edges, being careful not to smudge the cut itself.

A BLACK EYE

1. Dip your finger in the purple face paint and draw a ring under your eye, close to your nose. Dab your finger in the black face paint and add an extra-dark shadow below this ring, around the bone of your eye socket.

2. Add some red makeup to your eyelid and dot it into both corners of the eyelid. Blend some purple and blue along your eyebrow line so it looks like the "bruise" is starting to show.

3. Smudge some yellow into your brow bone and the top of your cheek, to give the impression of swelling.

4. Blend in a bit of green around the edges for a bruise that looks a few days old.

5. As a final touch, create the effect of cuts and scrapes by loading a sponge with red and dabbing it around your eye.

AN INJURED ARM

To match your amazing facial disguise, give yourself the appearance of an additional injury by wearing a sling. Once you have created your sling, simply slip your arm in and out of it whenever you need to.

1. Fold your fabric square in half to make a triangle. Put one end of the "sling" around one side of your neck and fold the rest of the fabric around the opposite arm, so that your arm is covered from elbow to wrist.

2. Lift the bottom corner and knot it to the corner behind your neck. Fold over the loose corner at your elbow and secure it with the safety pin.

Remember to look nervous if anyone comes too close to your arm—as though it might really hurt.

WALK WITH A LIMP

The finishing touch to your disguise is learning how to walk with a convincing limp. Put a small stone in one of your shoes to remind you which foot is supposed to be hurt. Your steps should be uneven, with the injured foot spending as little time as possible on the ground. Use the space around you for extra effect—hold onto a wall for support and wince occasionally to emphasize how much it "hurts."

You can use all these techniques to gain the complete accident-victim effect, or just try one at a time. Practice until you get the effects just right.

HOW TO SOLVE
THE DECRYPTION TEST

If you or your agents need extra help with the test on page 121, here are some clues to point you in the right direction.

1. Qeb pmv jxpqbo fp lrqpqxkafkd.

If "B" is "E," what might "X" be? Try writing out the alphabet and replacing these letters.

Translation: The spy master is outstanding.

2. Ztte je iwt vdds ldgz, ndj'gt vtiixcv qtiitg paa iwt ixbt.

Which letter might "T" be? It is a very popular letter. Write out the alphabet again and try a substitution code.

Translation: Keep up the good work, you're getting better all the time.

3. Svzwjfzigvih szh yvvm rmezwvw—wl mlg zkkilzxs.

What would happen if you reversed the alphabet? Try starting switching "A" with "Z" and working backward.

Translation: Headquarters has been invaded—do not approach.

4. Rednfiltratei neeber sahed ginred reyps ruore.

Remember the Switch-Up code on page 50? Apply those rules to this code to read this important warning.

Translation: Our spy ring has been infiltrated.

5. Maxx buva, kuo era vum e weqpar cuba-draeyar.

If you make the code wheel on pages 77–80 you'll be a code-breaking king!

Translation: Well done, you are now a master code-breaker.

AN A–Z OF SPY SPEAK

Agent—a spy

Call sign—radio code name

Camouflage—disguising yourself or an object to hide it

Cipher—a code

Code name—your secret "spy name"

Contact—the person you speak to about a mission

Dead-letter drop—the place where you leave your messages for other spies

Debriefing—discussing the mission after it's over

Decipher—to break a code

Dossier—your documents about a mission

Double agent—an agent secretly working for the enemy

Encoding/encryption—to conceal a message in a code

Espionage—spying

Field agent—a spy who goes out on missions

Go-between—the contact between field agents and the spy master

HQ—short for headquarters

Incognito—hiding your real identity

Infiltrate—sneakily gain access to another spy ring

Intelligence—information on your mission or target

Mark—the target who you are following

Operation—the spy ring's mission or plan

Recon—short for a reconnaissance mission (a mission where you're trying to gain information)

Rendezvous—a meeting with another spy

Shadow—the spy following you

Spy master—the person in charge of the spy ring

Spy ring—a group of spies working together

Surveillance—observation of a particular target or mark

Tail—to follow someone

Target—the person you need to follow

Unfriendlies—enemies

HOW TO TRAIN A NEW RECRUIT

Throughout this book there are useful tests you can use to monitor your recruits' core spying abilities, as well as your own spying abilities.

Have your recruits make a copy of the chart below to record their scores. They should fill it in using their code names (see page 26) with marks out of ten for each test.

Make a record of their progress to see how they improve over time. Remember, just because a recruit starts off badly in some areas does not mean he won't make a useful team member in other areas.

TEST	CODE NAME	
	SCORE OUT OF TEN	
Memory test one		☐
Memory test two		☐
Memory test three (Pages 31-32)		☐
Obstacle course (Pages 40-42)		☐
Action challenge (Pages 60-62)		☐
Code-breaking (Pages 120-121)		☐